Read and EXPERIM

Experiments
with
LIGHT

Isabel Thomas

heinemann
raintree

To contact Capstone Global Library, please call
800-747-4992, or visit our web site www.capstonepub.com

Edited by Clare Lewis and Amanda Robbins
Designed by Steve Mead
Picture research by Eric Gohl
Production by Victoria Fitzgerald
Originated by Capstone Global Library Ltd
Printed and bound by CTPS in China

19 18 17 16 15 14
10 9 8 7 6 5 4 3 2 1

Library of Congress Cataloging-in-Publication Data

Thomas, Isabel, 1979- author.
  Experiments with light / Isabel Thomas.
    pages cm.—(Read and experiment)
  Summary: "Explore the world of light with engaging text,
real life examples and fun step-by-step experiments. This
book brings the science of light to life, explaining the con-
cepts then getting kids to be hands-on scientists!"—Provided
by publisher.
  Includes bibliographical references and index.
  ISBN 978-1-4109-6837-1 (hb)—ISBN 978-1-4109-7901-8 (pb)
ISBN 978-1-4109-6842-5 (ebooks) 1. Light—Experiments—Juvenile literature. 2. Light—Juvenile literature. I. Title.

  QC360.T46 2015
  535.078—dc23   2014016072

This book has been officially leveled by using the F&P Text
Level Gradient™ Leveling System.

Acknowledgments

We would like to thank the following for permission to
reproduce photographs: iStockphotos: Kali Nine LLC, 6;
Shutterstock: Basileus, 11, charnsitr, 7 (top), Marcel Clemens,
16 (bottom), Ozerov Alexander, 7 (bottom), Piotr Krzeslak, 10,
raysay, 23 (bottom)

All other photographs were created at Capstone Studio by
Karon Dubke.

We would like to thank Patrick O'Mahony for his invaluable
help in the preparation of this book.

Every effort has been made to contact copyright holders
of material reproduced in this book. Any omissions will
be rectified in subsequent printings if notice is given to
the publisher.

All the Internet addresses (URLs) given in this book were valid
at the time of going to press. However, due to the dynamic
nature of the Internet, some addresses may have changed, or
sites may have changed or ceased to exist since publication.
While the author and publisher regret any inconvenience this
may cause readers, no responsibility for any such changes can
be accepted by either the author or the publisher.

Safety instructions for adult helper

The experiments in this book should be planned and carried out with adult supervision. Certain steps should
only be carried out by an adult – these are indicated in the text. Always follow the instructions carefully, and
take extra care when using scissors (pg. 18 and pg. 24), mirrors (pg. 22 and pg. 24) and electrical devices
such as flashlights (pg. 8, pg. 12, pg. 18, pg. 22 and pg. 24). Never look at the Sun directly. The publisher
and author disclaim, to the maximum extent possible, all liability for any accidents, injuries or losses that may
occur as a result of the information or instructions in this book.

Contents

Some words are shown in bold, **like this**. You can find out what they mean by looking in the glossary.

Why Experiment?

What makes objects different colors? How do shadows form? Why can't we see ourselves in a mirror if we look at it from the side? You can answer all these questions by investigating light.

Scientists ask questions like these. They find the answers with the help of **experiments**.

Get your eyes ready! You'll need to observe your experiments carefully and record what you see.

An experiment is a test that has been carefully planned to help answer a question.

The experiments in this book will help you to understand what light is and how it behaves. You'll learn how to work like a scientist, and have lots of fun along the way!

IS IT A FAIR TEST?

Most experiments involve changing something to see what happens. Make sure you only change one thing, or **variable**, at a time. Then you will know that it was the variable you changed that made the difference. This is called a fair test.

WARNING! Ask an adult to help you plan and carry out each experiment. Follow the instructions carefully. Look out for this sign.

ADULT HELP

Follow these steps to work like a scientist:

Ask a question.

↓

Come up with an idea to test.

↓

Plan an experiment.

↓

What will you change?
What will you keep the same?
What will you measure?

↓

Make a **prediction**.

↓

Observe carefully.

↓

Work out what the results mean.

↓

Answer the question!

What Is Light?

Light is a form of **energy**. Our eyes detect light energy. This allows us to see all the objects and colors around us.

Where does light come from?

Many light objects are hot objects. Stars, flames, and electric lamps all give off light. As the light travels away, it transfers energy from the **light source** to its surroundings.

REAL WORLD SCIENCE

The Sun is Earth's nearest star, and our brightest light source. Energy from the Sun travels to Earth as light. As well as allowing us to see, it keeps the planet warm and helps plants to grow. We couldn't live without light.

The Moon looks bright, but it is not a light source. We can see the Moon because light from the Sun bounces off it and travels to our eyes.

Never look at the Sun directly, or through any kind of binoculars or telescope. You could damage your eyes forever and even go blind. !

Light is produced in other ways too. This **bioluminescent** jellyfish gives off light because of **chemical changes** inside its body.

We see light sources because the light they give off travels to our eyes. Most objects are not light sources. We only see them when light bounces off them toward our eyes.

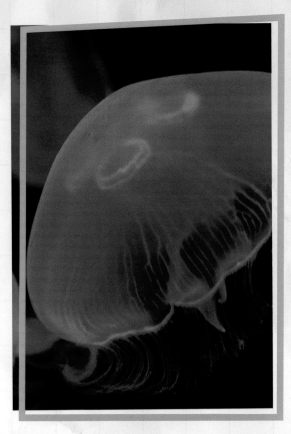

SEE THE SCIENCE ⤵

The light from a lamp or the Sun looks colorless or white but it is actually made up of seven different colors. When light is split into these colors we see a rainbow. Try splitting light by shining a beam of white light through a glass or a jug of water.

Sources of Light

Is every bright or shiny object a **light source**?
This **experiment** will help you to find out.

EQUIPMENT

- Cardboard box with tightly fitting lid
- Pencil
- Flashlight
- Small plastic toy
- Bright and shiny objects to test

Method

1 Put the toy spider in the box and close the lid. Carefully use the pencil to make a small hole in the side of the box.

2 Put your eye to the hole. What can you see?

Predict: Will you be able to see the spider if you put the light source in the box?

3 Now turn the flashlight on and put it inside the box with the spider. Replace the lid and look through the hole. Can you see the flashlight? Can you see the spider?

Predict: Which other objects are light sources?

4 Try out the other objects you have collected, one at a time. Draw a table to record your predictions and **observations**.

Object	Prediction: Will you be able to see the object in the closed box?	Observations: Can you see the object?
Flashlight		
Mirror		
Bike reflector		
LED		
Digital clock display		

5 **Analyze** your results. Which objects are light sources?

Conclusion

When you put a light source inside the box, light from the source also bounces off other things in the box and allows you to see them. Not every bright object is a light source though. Without light, we cannot see.

How Does Light Travel?

Light travels amazingly fast. The sunlight hitting Earth now has traveled 92 million miles (150 million kilometers) since it left the Sun eight minutes ago!

Most of light's journey from the Sun to Earth is through space, which is a **vacuum**. Light travels at about 186,000 miles (300,000 kilometers) per second in a vacuum. Light can also travel through other substances, such as air, but more slowly.

Light can pass through some materials, such as clear glass. We say these "see-through" materials are **transparent**.

In air, light travels about a million times faster than sound. This is why we see the lightning flash before we hear the sound it makes.

Other materials, such as wood and metal, stop light from passing through them. These materials are **opaque**.

Translucent materials, such as tissue paper, let some light through. These materials scatter the light, so shapes look fuzzy.

opaque

transparent

translucent

Different materials allow different amounts of light to pass through them.

SEE THE SCIENCE ⬇

When light travels from air into a liquid or solid, it slows down. This causes it to change direction. Try shining a narrow beam of light through a jar of jam. What happens to the light as it slows down? The light rays speed up again as they move from the jam back into air.

Glowing Lanterns

To make these glowing lanterns, you need a **translucent** material that will let some light through, but hide the **light source** inside. This **experiment** will help you to find the best material for your own spooky lantern.

EQUIPMENT

* Flashlight
* Box
* Range of different materials to test, such as cardboard, writing paper, tracing paper, acetate, tissue paper, foil, plastic wrap, crepe paper, different fabrics, or foam packaging
* Pencil

Method

1 Set up a flashlight in a box so it points upwards. Darken the room if you can. Can you see how the beam of light passes through the air and hits the ceiling?

2 Cut a square of your first material and use it to cover the flashlight. Look up at the ceiling. Can the light from the flashlight pass through the material? Record what you see. Is the paper **transparent**, translucent, or **opaque**?

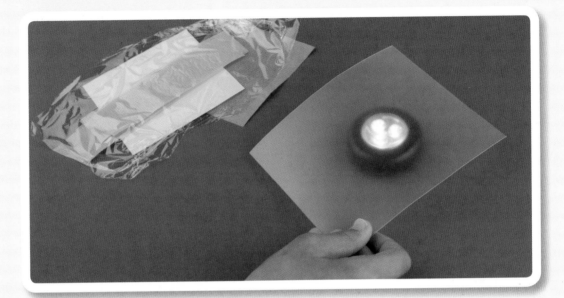

3 Add another layer of the same material. What happens? Record the number of sheets you have to add to block the light from the flashlight completely.

4 Repeat steps 2 and 3 using different materials and record what happens.

✓ IS IT A FAIR TEST?

You should only change the material itself. Everything else should stay the same. Is it a fair test if each material is a different thickness? How could you improve your experiment?

5 Draw a table to record your results. This will make it easier to compare them.

Material	How much light does it let through? All, some, or none?	How many layers before light blocked out?
None	All	
Paper		
Foil		

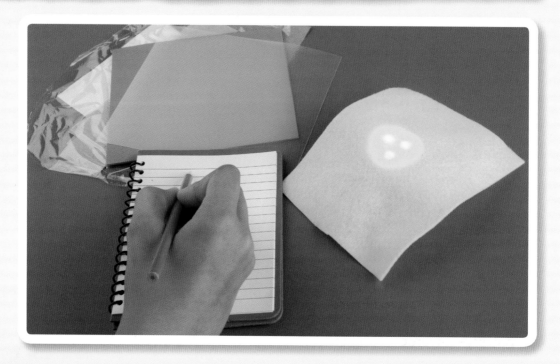

6 **Analyze** your results. Which materials are **opaque**? Which are **transparent**? Which are **translucent**? Which ones would be best for making a glowing paper lantern?

7 Draw a pattern on one side of a small box or paper bag. Ask an adult to help you cut it out. Stick a sheet of your chosen translucent material inside the box or bag, so it covers the cut-out pattern. Put a **light source** inside the lantern and watch it come to life!

Light your lanterns with a glow stick, flashlight, or battery-powered tea light.

Conclusion

Transparent materials let most light pass through them. We can see through them. Translucent objects let some light pass through them. We can't see through them. Opaque objects don't let any light pass through them. Translucent materials are best for making a glowing lantern. As you add more layers, translucent materials become less translucent.

What Are Shadows?

Light travels in a straight line. When it hits an **opaque** object, light can't pass through the object or bend around it. No light reaches the other side. A dark area called a shadow is formed.

A shadow is the same shape as the object blocking the light.

Light cannot pass through the dinosaur so a shadow forms.

Half of the Earth is always in shadow. The edge of the shadow is called the terminator. It's the line between day and night.

terminator

Your body casts a shadow when it blocks the path of light from the Sun, and stops the sunlight from hitting the ground.

As the Sun's position in the sky changes, the size and position of your shadow changes too. The higher the Sun is overhead, the shorter your shadow. It is shortest in the middle of the day. The lower the Sun is in the sky, the longer your shadow.

You can have fun with shadows!

SEE THE SCIENCE ⬇

On a sunny morning, stand a long stick in a pot of soil or sand. Use chalk to mark the stick's shadow. Repeat this every hour. Although the stick stays still, its shadow moves and changes shape. This is because the position of the **light source** (the Sun) changes.

Shadow play

A shadow is made when an object blocks the path of light. How can you change the size and shape of a shadow? **Experiment** with shadow puppets, and use what you discover to put on a show.

EQUIPMENT

- Cardboard and colored plastic
- Scissors
- Sticks or straws
- Bright flashlight
- Pale, flat background or wall
- Tape measure
- Toy figures

Method

1 Make shadow puppets by sticking cardboard characters on to straws or sticks. Light will not travel through the **opaque** card, but you can make eyes and other features by cutting holes.

> Be careful when using scissors and ask an adult to help you.

ADULT HELP

2 Place a flashlight on a table six feet (two meters) from a pale wall or sheet.

3 Hold a puppet three feet (one meter) from the torch. Does it cast a shadow on the wall? Measure and record the height of the shadow.

Predict: Will the shadow get bigger or smaller if you move the puppet away from the flashlight?

4 Move the puppet farther away from the flashlight. How big is the shadow now?

5 Move the puppet closer to the flashlight. How big is the shadow now? Copy and complete the table below to record your results. This will make it easier to compare them.

Distance of object from light source (inches)	Height of shadow (inches)
36	
48	
24	
12	
6	

Conclusion

You can change the size of a shadow by changing the distance between the object and the **light source**. Moving an object closer to the light source makes its shadow larger, because it blocks more of the light from the source. Moving an object farther from the light source makes its shadow smaller, because it blocks less of the light from the source.

Try these shadow challenges.

1 Can you change the shape of a shadow by turning the object? What happens when you turn a shadow puppet so its side faces the wall? Measure and record the height of the shadow.

2 Add a second **light source**. Can you give an object more than one shadow?

3 Stick colored plastic over the end of the torch to change the color of the light source. What happens to the shadows?

4 Make shadow puppets using **translucent** and **transparent** materials. Do they cast shadows? Are the shadows different from those cast by **opaque** objects?

5 Compare the shadows cast by large and small light sources (such as a desk lamp and a flashlight). How are they different?

6 Put on a shadow puppet play!
Use what you've found out about shadows to put on a puppet show. Can you make the shadows of your puppets and real people the same size?

Make a screen using a sheet hung from a clothes line. Shine light behind the screen and cast shadows on the screen, so the audience only sees the shadows.

How Do Mirrors Work?

When light hits an object, some light is absorbed. Some bounces off and changes direction. We say it has been **reflected**. Different surfaces reflect light in different ways.

Paper has a **dull**, rough surface. It reflects light, but scatters it in different directions. Some of the reflected light reaches your eyes wherever you stand. Smooth shiny surfaces reflect light without scattering it.

SEE THE SCIENCE ⬎

Be careful when using the mirror and flashlight.

!

Put a piece of paper on the floor. Shine a flashlight at the paper. Can you see a light spot where the beam hits the paper? Can you see it from different places? Replace the paper with a mirror. Shine the flashlight at the mirror. Can you see a light spot where the beam hits the mirror? Can you see it from anywhere in the room?

When you stand in front of a mirror, light reflected from your face bounces off the mirror and back toward your eyes without being scattered. You see an image of yourself in the mirror.

Why can't you see your reflection if you look at a mirror from the side? Rays of light hitting an object always bounce off at the same angle as they traveled toward it. Light hitting a mirror from the side will bounce off to the other side, like a ball kicked against a wall.

White light is made up of all the colors of the rainbow (see page 7). Objects look a certain colour because they reflect some of the colors and absorb the rest. This T-shirt absorbs every colour except red, and reflects only the red light to your eyes.

Goal!

Is it possible to **predict** where light will be **reflected** when it hits a mirror? Challenge yourself to a game of light soccer and find out.

EQUIPMENT

- Bright flashlight
- Black cardboard
- Scissors
- Tape
- White paper
- Mirror
- Colored pencils
- Ruler
- Protractor

Glass mirrors can be dangerous if you break them. Use plastic mirrors, or ask an adult to help you use a glass mirror.

ADULT HELP

Method

1 Stick two semi-circles of black card over the lightbulb of the flashlight, leaving a small gap in the middle (less than half an inch).

2 Draw a soccer field on a sheet of white paper.

3 Place the paper soccer field on a flat table, and set up a mirror where the red cross is in the picture. Darken the room.

Predict: Where will you need to put the flashlight to score a "goal" with light?

5 Use the flashlight to bounce a beam of light off the mirror and into the goal. Use a pencil to mark the path of the light beam before and after it hits the mirror.

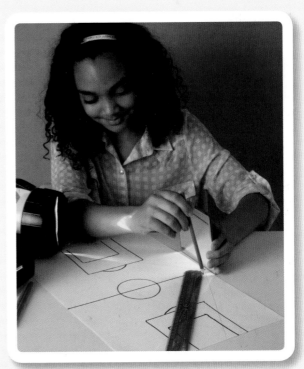

5 Use a protractor to measure the angle between each line and the center line on the field. Repeat step 4 to score goals from different starting points. Mark the path of each light beam before and after it hits the mirror. Use a different color for each goal.

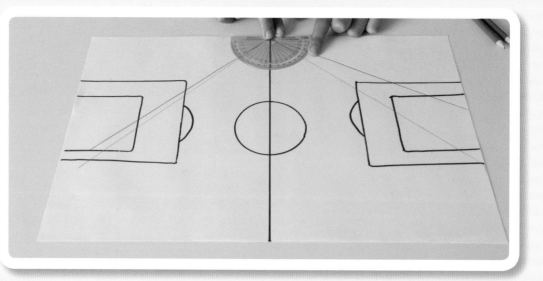

☑ IS IT A FAIR TEST?

Make sure you only change the position of the flashlight each time. The position of the mirror should stay the same.

6 Copy and complete the table to record your results.

Goal	Angle between the beam of light and the center line	Angle between reflected ray and dotted line
1		
2		
3		
4		

Can you score goals by changing the position of the mirror instead of the flashlight?

Conclusion

When light leaves the flashlight it travels in a straight line. When it hits the mirror, the light is **reflected** and travels away in a different direction. The light is reflected at exactly the same angle as it hits the mirror.

Plan Your Next Experiment

Experiments have helped you discover some amazing things about light. Just like you, scientists carry out experiments to answer questions and test ideas. Each experiment is planned carefully to make it a fair test.

YOU ASKED...

Can we see without light?

Which materials let light pass through them?

How do shadows change when we change the distance between an object and light source?

Can you **predict** where light will be **reflected** when it hits a mirror?

YOU FOUND OUT THAT...

- We see **light sources** when the light they give out enters our eyes.
- We can also see objects that don't give out their own light, but only when light from a source bounces off them towards our eyes. Without light, we cannot see.

- **Transparent** materials let most light pass through them. We can see through them clearly.
- **Translucent** materials let some light pass through them.
- **Opaque** materials do not let light travel through them. A shadow forms on the far side of the object.

- We see a shadow when an object blocks the path of light.
- The closer the light source is to the object, the larger the shadow.

- When light bounces off an object, we say it has been reflected.
- Each light ray is reflected at the same angle as it hits the object.
- A rough surface **scatters** reflected light in different directions.
- A smooth, shiny surface bounces the light in one direction.

Experiments also lead to new questions! Did you think of more questions about light? Can you plan experiments to help answer them?

Being a scientist and carrying out experiments is exciting. What will you discover next?

Glass mirrors can break into sharp pieces. Be careful and ask an adult to help you if you are planning an experiment using glass mirrors.

ADULT HELP

WHAT NEXT?

Do glow-in-the-dark materials reflect light or give out their own light? Plan an experiment to find out.

When light passes through a gap, does the size of the gap affect the light? Plan an experiment to find out.

Does the shadow of an object change if the light source is bigger or smaller than the object? Plan an experiment to find out.

What happens when you bounce a reflected beam of light off a second mirror? Does it change direction again? Plan an experiment to find out.

Glossary

analyze examine the results of an experiment carefully in order to explain what happened

bioluminescence when living things give off light

chemical change when different substance react together and change

dull not shiny

energy the power to make something happen

experiment procedure carried out to test an idea or answer a question

light source something that gives off energy as light

observation noting or measuring what you see, hear, smell or feel

opaque does not let light pass through

prediction best guess or estimate of what will happen, based on what you already know

reflect bounce light away without absorbing it or letting it pass through

reflected when light bounces off an object and changes direction

scatter reflect or bend light rays so they travel away in many different directions

translucent lets some light pass through, but not enough to see clearly through it

transparent lets light pass through; see-through

vacuum completely empty space

variable something that can be changed

Find Out More

Books

Spilsbury, Louise and Richard. *Light and Sound* (Essential Physical Science). Chicago: Heinemann Library, 2013

Riley, Peter. *Flash! Light and How We See Things.* London, UK: Franklin Watts, 2012

Winston, Robert. *Science Experiments.* London, UK: DK, 2011

Web sites

FactHound offers a safe, fun way to find internet sites related to this book. All of the sites on FactHound have been researched by our staff.

Here's all you do:
Visit www.facthound.com
Type in this code: 9781410968371

Index